HABITATS

Around the Poles

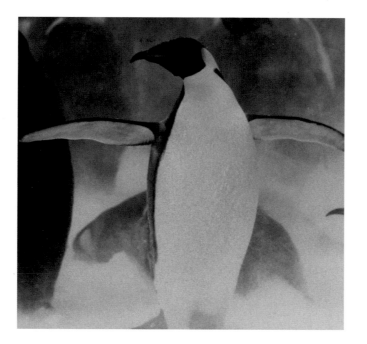

Robert Snedden

FRANKLIN WATTS
LONDON • SYDNEY

An Appleseed Editions book

First published in 2004 by Franklin Watts

Paperback edition 2007

Franklin Watts
338 Euston Road, London NW1 3BH

Franklin Watts Australia
Level 17/207 Kent Street, Sydney, NSW 2000

© 2004 Appleseed Editions Ltd
Well House, Friars Hill, Guestling, East Sussex TN35 4ET

Designed by Helen James

ISBN 978 0 7496 7641 4

Dewey Classification: 577' .0911

A CIP catalogue for this book is available from the British Library

Photographs by Donald Burnell, Corbis (Tom Bean, Brandon D. Cole, Tim Davis, Dan Guravich, Peter Johnson, George D. Lepp, Graham Neden; Ecoscene, Galen Rowell), Eugene G. Schultz, Tom Stack & Associates (Erwin & Peggy Bauer, Jeff Foott, John Gerlach, Thomas Kitchin, Joe McDonald, Dave Watts)

Printed and bound in Thailand

Franklin Watts is a division of Hachette Children's Books

Contents

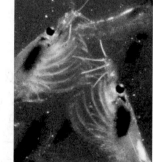

The ends of the Earth

The place where a living thing makes its home is called its **habitat**. A habitat can be as small as a damp place under a rotting log, or as big as the ocean. The biggest habitats, such as deserts, forests and mountains, are called **biomes**.

Polar biomes

The polar biomes are found around Earth's North and South Poles, in the Arctic and the Antarctic. The most obvious thing about these habitats is that they are very cold. The animals and plants that live there are **adapted** in various ways to living with the cold temperatures. Close to the poles,

conditions are so harsh, with permanent snow and ice, that no plants grow. Nothing can survive there for long.

The North Polar (Arctic) biome and the South Polar (Antarctic) biome differ from each other in a very important way.

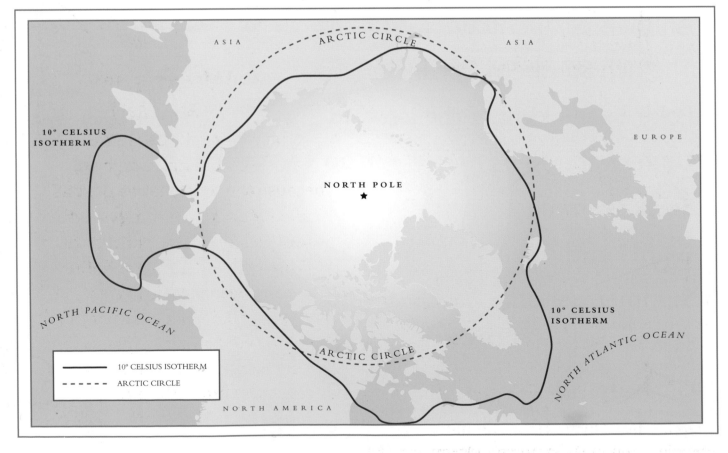

There is no land at the North Pole, just ice.

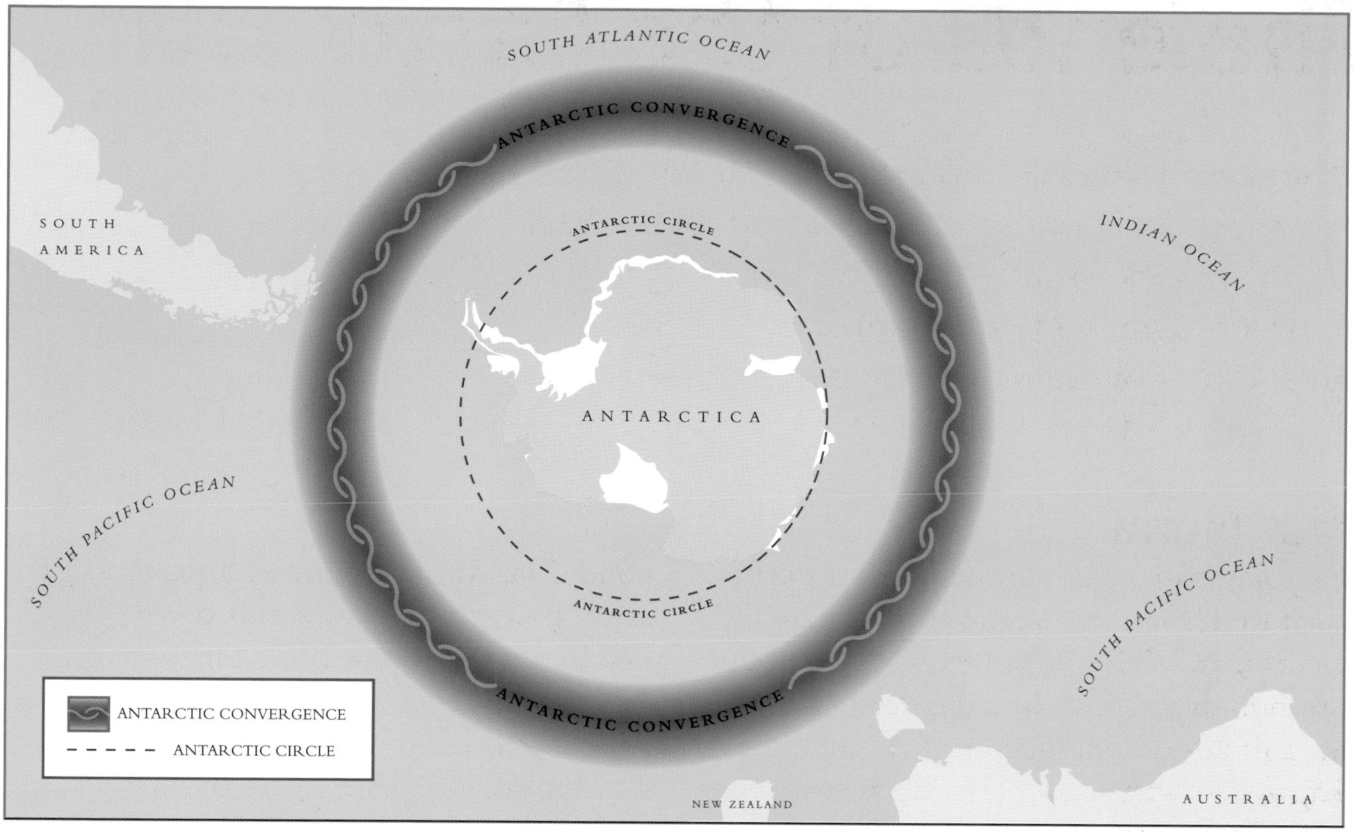
SOUTH ATLANTIC OCEAN
ANTARCTIC CONVERGENCE
SOUTH AMERICA
ANTARCTIC CIRCLE
INDIAN OCEAN
ANTARCTICA
SOUTH PACIFIC OCEAN
ANTARCTIC CIRCLE
SOUTH PACIFIC OCEAN
ANTARCTIC CONVERGENCE
ANTARCTIC CONVERGENCE
ANTARCTIC CIRCLE
NEW ZEALAND
AUSTRALIA

Antarctica is one of the Earth's large land masses, or continents.

The Arctic is a frozen ocean surrounded by land, whereas the Antarctic is a frozen continent surrounded by ocean. In the Arctic, specialized **predators** such as polar bears can live on animals such as fish and seals, which in turn find food in the waters beneath the ice. The Antarctic is a thick ice sheet lying on the continent of Antarctica. Nothing, apart from scientists, lives in the cold heart of Antarctica. Ice shelves lie along the edge of the continent, upon which large communities of birds such as penguins live. The birds feed on the abundant fish in the Antarctic Ocean.

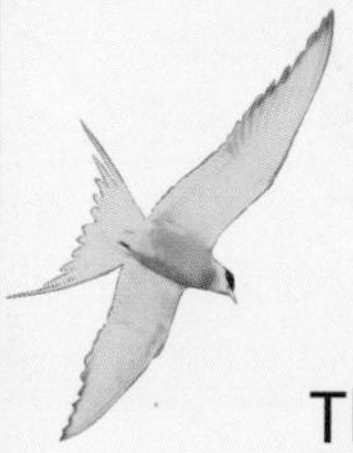

What's in a Name?

The word arctic comes from a Greek word meaning bear, because the **constellation** of stars called the Great Bear appears to revolve around the North Pole. (The Arctic is also home to the polar bear, but the ancient Greeks did not know that.) The word antarctic means opposite to the Arctic, and, coincidentally, there aren't any bears there.

Cold circles

Where exactly are the polar regions?
How do we mark them on a map?

▲ *Inside the Arctic Circle, the sun sinks lower and lower in the sky as winter approaches.*

The Arctic Circle

The southern boundary of the Arctic can be marked or defined in three ways. One is by the **Arctic Circle**, an imaginary line around the Earth. At this line, the sun does not set on the day of the **summer solstice** (usually 21 June) and does not rise on the day of the **winter solstice** (usually 21 December). North of the Arctic Circle, the periods of continuous daylight or night become progressively longer. At the North Pole, it is light for six months and dark for six months. The Arctic is also defined as the region north of the treeline, the northernmost limit of the forests. Trees do not grow further north because it is too cold.

Finally, the Arctic may be defined as an area within which the average daily summer temperature never rises above 10° Celsius. This line dips quite a bit below the Arctic Circle in some places. Southern Greenland is outside the

THE EXPANDING CONTINENT

The polar seas are so cold that floating chunks of ice, called pack ice, are common. During the autumn, the ocean around Antarctica starts to turn very cold. As winter progresses, the sea around the shore freezes at a rate of 4 kilometres per day. By September, the end of the Antarctic winter, about 20 million square kilometres of sea are covered by ice – an area twice the size of the United States. The continent of Antarctica itself is only 14 million square kilometres.

In the summer, the ice covering the Antarctic Ocean begins to melt and break up.

Arctic Circle, but it is still cold enough to be considered part of the polar region.

The Antarctic Circle

The northern boundary of the Antarctic can be marked in the same way as the southern boundary of the Arctic. However, the seasons are reversed. When it is summer in the Arctic, it is winter in the Antarctic. The sun does not rise on 21 June on the Antarctic Circle and it does not set on 21 December.

The northern boundary of the Southern Ocean, which surrounds Antarctica, lies where the layer of very cold water from the Antarctic suddenly dips under the warmer water from the oceans to the north. This band of water is called the Antarctic Convergence, and it marks the boundary of the southern polar region.

Weather forecast – cold!

The continent of Antarctica can be divided into three different **climate** zones: the interior, the coastal areas and the Antarctic Peninsula.

The interior

During the long, dark months of the Antarctic winter, the sun does not shine on the interior at all. The land of the interior is also very high, averaging about 2,500 metres. This adds to the chilliness of the conditions. The average temperature in an Antarctic year is -50° Celsius. During the short summer, which lasts from mid-December to mid-January, this rises to -30° Celsius.

The heart of Antarctica is far away from the ocean. It is very dry there. In fact, Antarctica is a frozen desert, receiving only about 50 millimetres of water – in the form of snow – every year. Fierce winds can whip up snow and ice from the surface into raging blizzards.

Scientists are the only living things in the heart of Antarctica. ▼

Around the coast

The coasts around Antarctica enjoy milder temperatures than the harsh interior. Average annual temperatures by the ocean range from -15 to -10° Celsius. During the summer months they can reach a bearable 9° Celsius. Close to the ocean, it is also much wetter. Every year, this region receives between 500 and 1,000 millimetres of water, mainly as snow. Heavy snowfalls can occur when storms pick up moisture from the sea and then blow inland. In the winter, as the amount of sunlight decreases, the sea ice grows and the coast cools.

 *Vegetation* is quite scarce on most of the Antarctic continent.

The Antarctic Peninsula

The most moderate climate on the continent is on the Antarctic Peninsula. This finger of land jutting out from the continent reaches much further north than the rest of Antarctica. The climate is warmer and wetter than elsewhere. Often the temperature rises above freezing for lengthy periods. At the northernmost end of the peninsula, rain is just as likely to fall as snow.

On the rocky shores of the Antarctic Peninsula birds and marine mammals, such as seals, nest and breed. Inland, plants such as grasses, lichens and mosses grow. However, life is hard here. Some of the world's strongest winds and its most ferocious storms can batter the peninsula for days – or even weeks – on end without ceasing.

Arctic climate

Like the Antarctic, at the other end of the world, the Arctic is cold and very dry. The North Polar biome is another frozen desert.

Not-so-sunny days

The sun never rises very high in the sky in the polar regions, which is why the Arctic is so cold. The rays of the sun strike the Earth at an angle which spreads out the warmth over a large area. At the same time, the sun's rays have to pass through a thicker slice of the Earth's **atmosphere**. This means that they lose a lot of energy on the way to the ground.

Warmth from the south

Arctic cold is not as severe as the Antarctic cold. Warm air and warm ocean currents flow to the Arctic from the south, making the climate there a little milder.

For six months of the year, the sun doesn't rise at all at the North Pole. If it wasn't for the warmth from the south, the temperature would plummet during the winter. The warm air brings moisture, and moist air forms clouds. These clouds act like a blanket and help to prevent a drop in temperature.

The aurora borealis, or northern lights, make a spectacular display in the Arctic winter sky. ▶

Arctic seasons

The Arctic year is divided into four seasons. Arctic winter, which starts in late September, is the period during which the sun is very low in the sky (or doesn't rise at all). This is, understandably, the coldest time of the year. Arctic spring is a warming–up period. The sun rises a little higher in the sky, and some of the ice over the ocean and in the frozen soil begins to melt. This is a slow process. Spring in the far north lasts until June.

Arctic summer is a short season. By the time the ice has melted and the ground is uncovered and begins to warm up, the sun is sinking lower in the sky once more. Although the days may be quite mild, night-time temperatures can drop below freezing. However, the average temperature stays above freezing throughout the summer days.

As winter begins to take hold in the Arctic, many animals, such as these snow geese, begin to leave for warmer places.

Summer is also the wettest time of year in the Arctic. Rivers thaw, and evaporating water from the land forms clouds in the sky. Even so, the amount of rainfall is small.

Summer in the far north starts to end in July, although it lasts until August or September further from the North Pole. The sun sinks lower in the sky every day. The ground receives less warming energy and starts to freeze. This cooling-down period is polar autumn. Eventually the sea freezes, and the Arctic is in the grip of winter once more.

Tundra – land of extremes

South of the true polar regions of the Arctic are the cold, treeless plains of the **tundra**. The word tundra comes from a Finnish word that means marshy plain. The tundra stretches from Alaska to Newfoundland in North America, and from northern Scandinavia to Siberia in Asia. If there were land north of Antarctica that would be tundra, too.

Permafrost

The ground surface of the tundra is wet and spongy. From a few centimetres beneath the surface, the soil of the tundra is permanently frozen to a depth of a metre or more. This frozen soil, called **permafrost**, makes it impossible for large-rooted plants such as trees to grow. The part of the ground that thaws in the summer is called the active layer. It is very wet because the water from the melted ice cannot drain away through the frozen permafrost layer below.

Tundra seasons

Winter on the tundra is long, dry and very cold. For six to eight months of the year, the average temperature remains below freezing. Days are short, clear and bright. The Siberian tundra is bitterly cold in winter, with temperatures often falling below –50° Celsius. It is not quite so cold on the North American tundra, but it is still very chilly!

Summer is short-lived. Only about two or three months of the year are free from frost.

When the snow and ice finally disappear for the summer, tundra plants burst into spectacular growth.

Snowy owls are important hunters of the tundra. Each owl eats about a dozen lemmings (a kind of rodent) a day.

The summer days are long and reasonably mild. On some days, it may be as warm as 18° Celsius, though the average monthly temperature stays below 10° Celsius. Most of the rain that falls on the tundra comes during the summer months.

The plants and animals of the tundra have to cope with a huge range of temperatures. The difference between winter low and summer high can be more than 60 degrees in central Siberia, though a range of 30 degrees is more common. This makes the tundra climate more extreme than that of any other biome.

Tundra life

The tundra does not have the rich variety of life of other biomes. Simple plants, such as lichens, grasses, mosses and a few dwarf shrubs, grow on the tundra. Tundra plant-eaters include big animals such as caribou and musk oxen, as well as smaller animals such as voles and lemmings. Not only do these plant-eaters have to survive the climate, they also have to deal with tundra **carnivores**, including polar bears, Arctic foxes and wolves. Most tundra birds are only part-time inhabitants. They make good use of their flying abilities and **migrate** to warmer places to avoid the winter. No **reptiles** or **amphibians** live on the tundra. They could not survive in such cold conditions.

Animals of the Arctic

When people think of Arctic animals, most imagine polar bears moving across the frozen sea, or herds of reindeer or caribou roaming the treeless tundra. Or they may think of shaggy musk oxen huddled together for warmth, their horns turned out to protect them from prowling wolves.

All these large animals make their homes in the Arctic. Smaller residents include foxes, hares, squirrels and rodents such as voles and lemmings. The seas surrounding the Arctic are full of fish such as cod and salmon, which swim in the cold ocean below the ice cap. Whales, sea lions, walruses and seals all arrive in the spring to feed on the fish.

Insects that survive the winter as eggs in the frozen ground emerge in black, biting clouds in the spring that can make life miserable for larger animals. Birds are attracted to the tundra in huge numbers to feast on the insects and to nest and raise their chicks. These birds include plovers, larks, finches, ducks and geese.

Arctic foxes are well adapted to the cold. They even have fur on the bottom of their feet. ▶

Keeping warm

Arctic animals have two adaptations for dealing with the cold – fat and fur. As winter approaches, animals build up their fat reserves. An adult caribou carries

▲ *If musk oxen are attacked, they form a circle, with the young protected in the middle.*

a layer of fat over its back that can make up a sixth of its total body weight. As well as keeping the caribou warm, the fat layer is a useful energy reserve for when food is hard to find. Arctic foxes have dense winter coats that protect them from the cold. The musk ox has both a shaggy coat of long hair that hangs straight to the ground and a layer of insulating fat.

The Arctic fox's coat changes from brownish-grey to white as winter approaches. This helps to **camouflage** the fox against the snow. But the coat gives the fox another advantage. The pigment inside the hair that gives the coat its colour in summer disappears and is replaced by air. These air-filled hairs act as a valuable insulating layer, keeping the fox warm.

Surviving the cold seas

Objects in the water, including living things, lose heat 25 times faster than in the air. This is one reason it is so dangerous for someone to fall from a ship into the cold sea. The sea animals of the Arctic, such as seals and beluga whales, are kept warm by thick layers of insulating **blubber** just under their skin. A whale's blubber layer can be half a metre thick. Arctic fish have a substance in their blood that acts like the antifreeze drivers put in their car engines to protect them against the winter cold. This stops the animals' blood freezing in the sub-zero cold of the deep ocean.

The rich Southern Ocean

The Antarctic continent is a harsh environment. Only a few simple plants and some microscopic organisms live inland. Most of the life of Antarctica clusters around the coast or in the Southern Ocean that surrounds the continent.

The waters around Antarctica are constantly on the move. As the cold waters of the Southern Ocean meet the warm waters of the Atlantic, Pacific and Indian Oceans, the cold water sinks beneath the warm water. This is the Antarctic Convergence. The sinking cold water makes **minerals** and **nutrients** well up from the ocean floor.

Tiny mouthfuls

Microscopic organisms called phytoplankton, which are a bit like tiny, floating plants, use the nutrients brought up from the bottom by the cold water flow. They use the energy of the sun to make their food from carbon dioxide and water. The food they make and store within themselves provides a supply of energy for all the bigger living things in the Antarctic. Phytoplankton are the first link in the Antarctic **food chain**.

Tiny, shrimp-like krill are one of the next links in the chain. There are huge numbers of these small animals, which measure about 6 centimetres long. They feast on phytoplankton. At their most plentiful, the world's population of krill outweighs the human race about five to six times.

These shrimp-like creatures are an important food source for Antarctic wildlife.

Big eaters

Energy is always lost as it passes from one animal to another along a food chain. When big Arctic animals eat the tiny krill, they are right at the start of the food chain. This means they are close to the primary energy source – the phytoplankton. Little energy is lost in a short Antarctic food chain. This is why the Antarctic Ocean can support such a large population of big animals such as whales. Even so, a whale has to eat a lot of krill. A blue whale feeding in the Southern Ocean can consume more than 4 tonnes of krill in one day!

Krill are one of the most important links in the Antarctic food chain, providing food for fish, whales and penguins. All other wildlife in the Antarctic either eat krill or eat something else that eats krill.

Blue whales, the largest living animals in the world, eat huge quantities of krill in the waters of the Southern Ocean. ▼

Polar bear – king of the ice

The polar bear, fearless hunter of the Arctic **pack ice**, is probably the most impressive polar animal. It is supremely well adapted to its environment.

The polar bear is the world's largest land carnivore. An adult male bear can measure 3 metres in length and weigh as much as 800 kilograms, which is about the same as a small car. Females are about half the size, but they are still fierce and capable **predators**.

Arctic adaptations

The thick winter coat of the polar bear, with its dense underfur, protects the bear against the Arctic cold. The polar bear's fur is also water repellent. When a bear comes out of the water, it shakes itself dry like a dog after a swim. Polar bear hair reflects

Polar bears sometimes use blocks of ice as pillows when they sleep.

the warmth from the sun down to the animal's heat-absorbing black skin. A thick layer of fat beneath the skin completes the bear's protection.

The polar bear's white fur is used for camouflage as well as warming. Polar bears are very good at taking seals by surprise. A hunting polar bear sniffs the air with its keen nose. It can pick up the scent of a seal breathing hole hidden a metre below the ice and snow more than a kilometre away.

The soles of polar bears' feet have small bumps and dents that act like suction cups. These bumps grip the ice and help to stop the bears slipping and sliding. Polar bears walk fairly slowly across the ice. They don't like to run; they are so well insulated that they overheat very easily.

Polar bears are strong swimmers. They use their powerful front paws to row themselves through the water. Their back paws act as rudders, helping them steer.

Where to find a polar bear

There are probably between 25,000 and 30,000 polar bears in the world. They live along the Arctic coast and among the islands of the Arctic Ocean. Small numbers roam the pack ice over the ocean, but they do not stray as far north as the North Pole.

A few polar bears wander as far south as Newfoundland.

Polar bears prefer places where the ice is broken up by areas of open water. This is where they are most likely to find the seals they like to eat. In the spring, female polar bears take their cubs on hunts for newborn seals. The females use their powerful paws to smash their way into the seals' lairs. Polar bears also lie in wait on the ice beside seal breathing holes. When seals come up for air, the bears flip them out on to the ice, and kill them with a single blow.

In the summer, when the pack ice melts, polar bears have to come ashore. This means they cannot hunt seals and have to live on their reserves of fat until the sea freezes again. Some eat berries to sustain themselves. Others try to catch seabirds.

▼ *Polar bears are agile hunters.*

Underwater fliers

Think of the Antarctic and it's hard not to think of penguins, too. They may look comical waddling upright on the ice in their black and white feathers, but penguins are ideally suited to life on the edge of the Antarctic. In the water, these awkward-looking birds are swift and deadly hunters.

Where do penguins live?

Two types of penguin, the Adélie and the emperor penguin, live only in Antarctica. Most penguins live throughout the islands of the Southern Ocean and along the southern coastlines of Africa, South America and Australia.

The Galápagos penguin lives on the Galápagos islands just to the north of the **equator**. Emperor and king penguins have been known to go on hunting trips lasting a month and covering more than 1,500 kilometres of ocean.

Penguins on parade

There are 17 different types of penguins, and they are all built along the same lines. This is because they all have a similar lifestyle and so are adapted in the same way. All penguins have sleek, **streamlined** bodies with dark backs and white bellies. This colour scheme stands out on land, but it is ideally suited to life in the water. Seen from above, the penguin blends in with the dark sea. Seen from below, it blends with the bright sky.

Penguins cannot fly although they have wings. The penguin's wings have evolved into paddle-like flippers. Together with the bird's rudder-like, stubby tail and its broad feet, the wings allow the penguin to swim with great skill underwater. The penguin's swimming ability also helps it to escape from bigger predators

such as killer whales and leopard seals. Other birds have lightweight bones, but the penguin's bones are solid and heavy. This is an adaptation that allows them to dive deep in search of fish and shrimp. Many penguins spend four-fifths of their lives in the water and often dive 300 metres or more beneath the surface in search of food.

◀ *Emperor penguins head south to their breeding grounds in the heart of the Antarctic winter, enduring fierce winds and bitterly cold temperatures.*

LITTLE AND LARGE

The little blue penguin of New Zealand and Australia is the world's smallest penguin, measuring just 45 centimetres tall and weighing only a kilogram. The world's largest penguin is the emperor, which stands more than a metre tall and weighs around 40 kilograms.

Sleek swimmers

Most of the world's seals live in the Antarctic or the Arctic. They are one of the few animals which live in both places, though there are many more seals in the south polar region than in the north.

Fin-footed animals

Seals, along with their close relatives the sea lions and walruses, are called fin-footed animals because their front and back legs resemble flippers. This is an adaptation to a life spent mainly swimming in the sea.

Although they can spend long periods of time underwater, seals are **mammals** and, like all mammals, they breathe air. Seals and other fin-foots do spend some time on land, occasionally coming ashore to rest. Every year large numbers of seals come to the shore or the edge of the sea ice to give birth to their young.

Streamlined swimmers

On shore, seals move awkwardly, flopping along on their bellies. They pull themselves along with their front flippers, as they cannot use their back flippers on land. In the sea, however, they move very differently.

In the water, seals use their back flippers to propel themselves forwards. Swimming seals are streamlined torpedoes which cut effortlessly through the water. Seals' bodies have a thick layer of fat called blubber just under the skin. This acts as an excellent insulating layer which keep seals warm,

The walrus is a long-tusked relative of the seal that lives amid the sea ice of the Arctic Ocean.

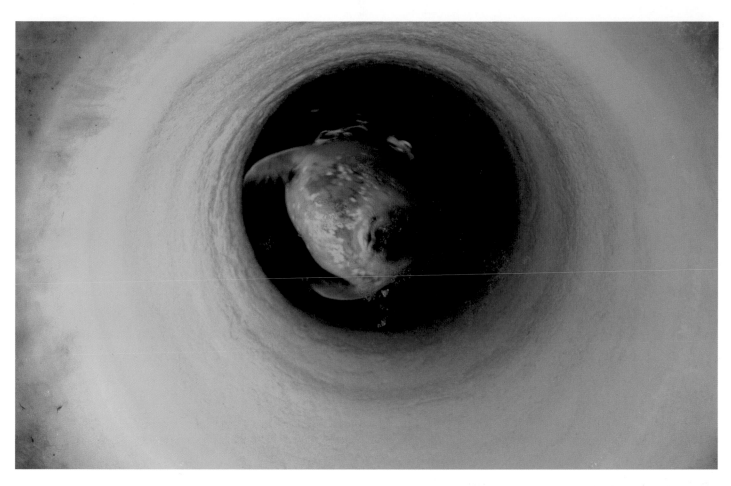

and it also helps to give seals their streamlined shape.

Seals find their **prey** of shrimp, fish and squid in the water by using their sensitive whiskers to detect vibrations in the water. Their large eyes also give them a keen sense of sight. And some seals can hear more than ten times better underwater than on land!

Like all mammals, seals need air to breathe. They keep blowholes open in the ice for this purpose.

Antarctic seals

Seals live throughout the Antarctic. About half the world's seals live there. One reason there are so many more seals in Antarctica than in the Arctic is that the Antarctic Ocean has such a rich food supply. The seals of Antarctica eat krill, which live in huge numbers in the Southern Ocean. Another reason is that there are fewer seal hunters – such as polar bears or humans – in the Antarctic. True Antarctic seals, which live around the continent of Antarctica, are the Weddell seal, the Ross seal, the crabeater seal and the leopard seal.

TOP DIVERS
The Weddell seal can reach depths of more than 500 metres and stay underwater for more than an hour.

Giants of the sea

Whales may be the most magnificent creatures in the world's oceans. Many of them live in polar waters for at least part of the year.

Toothed and baleen

Whales are divided into two groups: toothed and baleen. Toothed whales catch and eat other ocean dwellers such as squid, fish, penguins and seals with their teeth. Baleen whales have no teeth. Instead, they have a comb-like structure that they use to filter small animals such as krill from the water. Toothed whales are smaller than baleen whales. The orca (killer whale) and the sperm whale are the only toothed whales found in the Antarctic. Antarctic baleen whales include the blue, fin, humpback, minke, sei and southern right.

In the Arctic, belugas and narwhals (both toothed whales) and bowheads (a baleen whale) live year-round in the polar seas. Orcas arrive in the summer, following migrating seals and other whales north as the ice opens up, but they are not considered to be true Arctic whales because they do not spend the winter there.

Living in the water

Whales' sleek, streamlined bodies are ideally adapted to a life moving through the water.

The California grey whale is one of the most commonly seen whales off the west coast of the United States as it makes its way to and from its Arctic feeding grounds.

Whales, and their close relatives dolphins and porpoises, are the only mammals, other than manatees, that never leave the water. They are also the only mammals that live in the deep oceans. Like all mammals, whales are warm-blooded, and whale mothers provide milk for their young. Although they can dive deep and stay underwater for an hour or more, whales have lungs and must breathe air to stay alive. They periodically rise to the surface of the ocean to breathe through their blowholes. A whale's blowhole, on top of its head, is its nostril. The whale closes off its blowhole when it dives.

Many whales migrate long distances. Antarctic whales spend the summer feeding in the rich waters of the Southern Ocean before heading off in the winter months to the warmer northern waters to breed and give birth to their young. The California grey whale is a summer visitor to the Arctic. It makes a round trip of more than 18,000 kilometres from its breeding grounds near Baja California in Mexico, to its summer feeding grounds in the Bering Sea (between Alaska and Russia) and back again. No other mammal migrates further.

Orcas, or killer whales, live in all the world's oceans, particularly around the Arctic and Antarctic, where they catch and eat seals.

WHICH WAY?
Fish swim by moving their tails to the left and right. Whales swim by moving their tail flippers, or flukes, up and down.

Summer visitors

When the long polar winter comes to an end, and the brief summer begins, millions of birds arrive in the polar regions to breed. Perhaps a hundred million or more breed along the coast and offshore islands of Antarctica, including huge colonies of penguins and long-distance fliers such as albatrosses, skuas and petrels.

Antarctic seabirds have a number of adaptations to help them stay warm in the cold climate. They have waterproof feathers, a layer of fat just under their skin, and large, compact bodies that don't lose heat very quickly.

Even in the summer there is not much snow-free ground in the Antarctic. This forces seabirds to form large colonies on the few patches of bare ground that are suitable for nesting. During the Antarctic summer, there is an abundance of food for the birds to eat. The ocean is full of fish, shrimp, squid and other marine creatures. Because the summer is so short, chicks (young birds) develop quickly and can soon fend for themselves. When winter returns, the birds migrate north to find warmer conditions.

▼ *Skuas are similar to seagulls, but bigger and more aggressive. They are superb fliers.*

The Arctic tern is the world's greatest long-distance traveller.

Breeding grounds

Just eight **species** of birds live in the Arctic all the year round. During the summer, they are joined by 150 others. Many species of geese, such as the grey goose, the Canada goose and the barnacle goose, return to the Arctic every summer to breed. There they can feed on the summer plants and the countless insects and other small creatures that emerge for the brief season. Another advantage for the geese is that there are fewer predators in the far north.

The problem the geese face is the same as that faced by the southern birds: summer is very short. The geese must nest, lay their eggs and raise their young in just two or three months.

Champion traveller

The Arctic tern is a remarkable bird that might just as easily be called the Antarctic tern. Every year this small, 300 gram bird makes the longest journey of any animal in the world. The Arctic tern breeds in the tundra on the edge of the Arctic and then sets off on a journey of nearly 18,000 kilometres to the edge of the Antarctic ice at the other end of the world. Every year it covers a total of more than 35,000 kilometres. Not surprisingly, almost all the tern's life is spent in the air. It eats small fish and krill, swooping down to the water to catch them in its beak.

TO THE MOON – AND BACK!

An Arctic tern might live to be 20 years old. Throughout its life, it might fly a distance which is equivalent to flying to the moon and back again!

The poles in peril?

The polar regions are the harshest environments on the planet. Despite this, a rich variety of life has adapted to the harsh conditions there. Polar life is in a delicate balance with the cold climate, and any change can have a severe effect on it.

Disappearing bears

The mighty hunters of the Arctic – polar bears – are losing weight. They have less to eat, fewer cubs are born and some cubs don't survive because their mothers can't feed them. What's happening to the bears?

The answer is **global warming**. As temperatures rise worldwide, the Arctic ice cap melts. Polar bears do most of their hunting for seals on the sea ice, so for part of the year, when the summer sun melts the ice, the bears have to come ashore. This is a hungry time for the bears, and the hungry times are growing longer as the ice begins to melt earlier in the year. If the ice disappears completely, the bears will lose their habitat and, consequently, their lives.

Save the bears

Every time **fossil fuels** such as coal, oil and gas are burned, **greenhouse gases** are released into the atmosphere. Many scientists believe that these gases trap the sun's heat, causing the Earth to warm up. Some say that simple actions such as putting on a jumper, turning down the heating in buildings, or using fuel-efficient public transport could help keep the planet's temperature from rising. Not everyone agrees, though. Some scientists believe that the increase in the Earth's temperature is simply part of a natural cycle of climate change.

As their habitat continues to disappear, polar bears face an uncertain future. ▼

Hole in the sky

High in the atmosphere lies a layer of gas called ozone. This gas absorbs harmful **radiation** from the sun before it reaches the Earth's surface. In recent years, scientists have discovered a hole in the ozone layer over Antarctica. The hole was caused by the release of chemicals used in refrigerators and aerosol cans. Scientists believe that radiation streaming through the hole is killing large numbers of fish eggs and larvae on the surface of the Southern Ocean and reducing the number of phytoplankton by about 15 per cent. Phytoplankton feed krill, and krill feed everything else. It is easy to see how serious this could be not just for the Antarctic, but the rest of the world as well.

But there is hope. Some scientists believe that if gas emissions are reduced, the hole over Antarctica could repair itself by

Weather balloons are used to check conditions in the atmosphere above Antarctica.

about 2100. This would help to restore fish and phytoplankton to more normal levels and could, in turn, make the region's future less uncertain.

VANISHING ICE CAP

Since 1978, the Arctic ice cap has shrunk by an average of 33,800 square kilometres every year. By the end of the 20th century, an area almost as big as France and Italy together had disappeared.

Glossary

adapted Suited to life in a particular environment.

amphibians Types of animals, such as frogs and toads, with soft, moist skin, that spend at least part of their lives in water.

Arctic Circle An imaginary line around the north polar regions.

atmosphere The layer of gases that surrounds the Earth.

biomes Large areas of the environment with distinctive climates and plant types; examples include forests, mountains and deserts.

blubber The layer of fat that insulates whales from the cold of the ocean.

camouflage To make something difficult to see because it is the same colour or shape as the background.

carnivores Animals that feed on other animals; meat-eaters.

climate The general weather conditions in a particular area.

constellation A pattern of stars in the sky.

equator An imaginary line that runs around the middle of the Earth, dividing it into the northern and southern hemispheres.

food chain A feeding relationship between living things. Food chains begin with organisms such as green plants that can make their own food. Next come animals that eat the plants, then animals that eat the plant-eaters.

fossil fuels Fuels such as coal, crude oil and natural gas that are formed from the remains of plants and animals that lived millions of years ago.

global warming The rise in the average temperature of the Earth, thought to be the result of the increasing amount of greenhouse gases in the atmosphere.

greenhouse gases Gases in the atmosphere that trap heat as it rises from the surface of the Earth, like the glass in a greenhouse, causing the atmosphere to be warmer than it would be if the heat escaped into space.

habitat The place where a living thing makes its home; the environment that it is adapted to survive in.

mammals Animals that are warm-blooded and usually have hair on their skin, including humans and bears. Female mammals produce milk to feed their young.

migrate To move from one place to another in search of better living conditions.

minerals Chemicals needed as part of a healthy diet. Different minerals are used in a variety of ways, including growth and the regulation of the body's activities.

nutrients Another word for food – all the things needed for a balanced diet which provides energy and raw materials for the growth and maintenance of the organism.

pack ice Large pieces of ice that float in the cold seas of the polar regions.

permafrost A layer of soil that is permanently frozen.

predators Animals that catch and eat other animals for food.

prey Animals that are caught and eaten by predators.

radiation Energy that travels from one place to another as particles, such as those given off by radioactive materials, or waves, such as light and heat.

reptiles Cold-blooded animals, including snakes and lizards, with dry, scaly skin. Most lay soft-shelled eggs and live on land.

species A group of living things with the same general appearance and behaviour, which can breed together to produce fertile offspring.

streamlined Shaped to allow movement through air or water with minimum resistance.

summer solstice The time of year when the daylight hours are longest. This is often 21 June in the northern hemisphere.

tundra A region of the cold north where there is a layer of permafrost beneath the topsoil, few trees can grow and the vegetation is mainly grasses and mosses.

vegetation The plant life in an area.

winter solstice The time of year when the daylight hours are shortest. This is often 21 December in the northern hemisphere.

Index